Meet the
NEW ORLEANS
SAINTS

BY
ZACK BURGESS

NORWOOD HOUSE 🏠 PRESS

CHICAGO, ILLINOIS

NORWOOD HOUSE ◼ PRESS

P.O. Box 316598 • Chicago, Illinois 60631
For more information about Norwood House Press please visit our website at
www.norwoodhousepress.com or call 866-565-2900.

Photo Credits:
All photos courtesy of Associated Press, except for the following: Topps, Inc. (6, 10 top, 11 top & middle),
Black Book Archives (7, 15, 18, 23), NFLPA (10 bottom), Fleer Corp. (11 bottom).

Cover Photo: Bill Haber/Associated Press

The football memorabilia photographed for this book is part of the authors' collection. The collectibles used
for artistic background purposes in this series were manufactured by many different card companies—
including Bowman, Donruss, Fleer, Leaf, O-Pee-Chee, Pacific, Panini America, Philadelphia Chewing Gum,
Pinnacle, Pro Line, Pro Set, Score, Topps, and Upper Deck—as well as several food brands, including
Crane's, Hostess, Kellogg's, McDonald's and Post.

Designer: Ron Jaffe
Series Editors: Mike Kennedy and Mark Stewart
Project Management: Black Book Partners, LLC.
Editorial Production: Lisa Walsh

LIBRARY OF CONGRESS CATALOGING-IN-PUBLICATION DATA
Names: Burgess, Zack.
Title: Meet the New Orleans Saints / by Zack Burgess.
Description: Chicago, Illinois : Norwood House Press, [2016] | Series: Big
picture sports | Includes bibliographical references and index. |
Audience: Grade: K to Grade 3.
Identifiers: LCCN 2015026316| ISBN 9781599537474 (Library Edition : alk.
paper) | ISBN 9781603578509 (eBook)
Subjects: LCSH: New Orleans Saints (Football team)--Miscellanea--Juvenile
literature.
Classification: LCC GV956.N366 B87 2016 | DDC 796.332/640976335--dc23
LC record available at http://lccn.loc.gov/2015026316

288N—072016
Manufactured in the United States of America in North Mankato, Minnesota

CONTENTS

Words in **bold type** are defined on page 24.

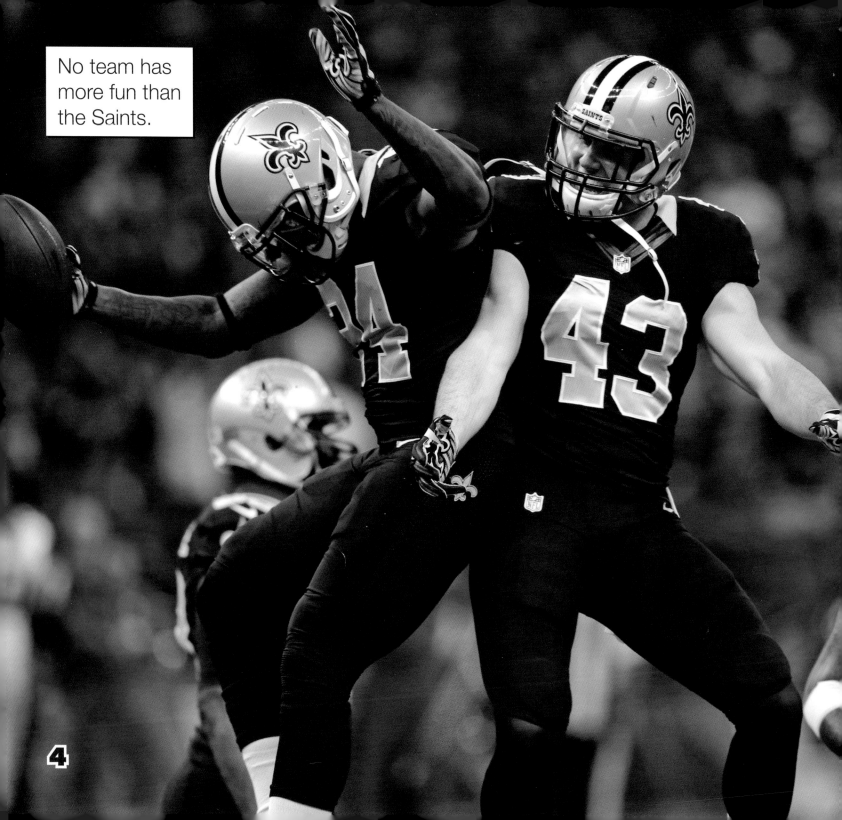

No team has more fun than the Saints.

CALL ME A SAINT

The people of New Orleans love jazz music. The Saints are named after the jazz song, "When the Saints Come Marching In." In 2005, a deadly hurricane struck New Orleans. The Saints lifted the city's spirits. Ever since, the players have been celebrated as heroes.

TIME MACHINE

The Saints played their first season in the National Football League (NFL) in 1967. Their first star was quarterback **Archie Manning**. Other talented passers followed him. Drew Brees was the best. He led the Saints to their first NFL championship, in 2009.

ARCHIE MANNING   QUARTERBACK
SAINTS

Drew Brees spots an open receiver.

The Louisiana Superdome is a huge building.

Best Seat in the House

The Saints play in the Louisiana Superdome. It is one of the largest domed stadiums in the world. It is also one of the noisiest. Win or lose, Saints fans can make the Superdome feel like one big party.

SHOE BOX

The trading cards on these pages show some of the best Saints ever.

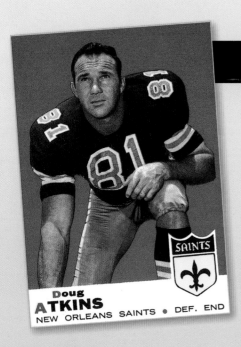

DOUG ATKINS

DEFENSIVE END · 1967-1969

Doug was the Saints' best pass rusher in their early years. He was voted into the **Hall of Fame** in 1982.

ARCHIE MANNING

QUARTERBACK · 1971-1982

Saints fans loved watching Archie make exciting plays. Eli and Peyton Manning are his sons.

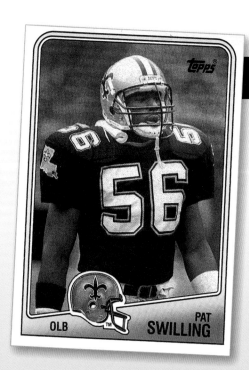

PAT SWILLING

LINEBACKER · 1986-1992

Pat was a leader of the team's famous "Dome Patrol." Sam Mills, Rickey Jackson, and Vaughan Johnson played beside him.

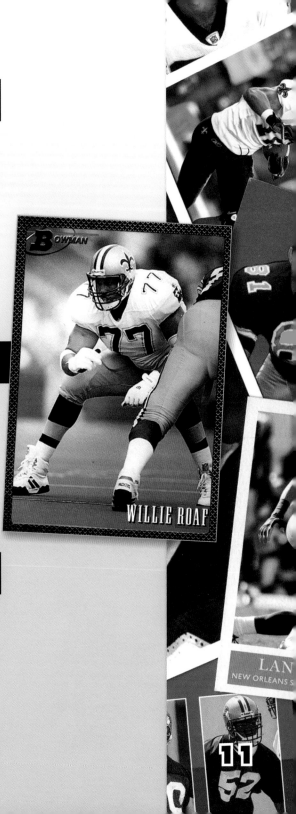

WILLIE ROAF

OFFENSIVE TACKLE · 1993-2001

Willie was one of the best blockers in the NFL. He was an **All-Pro** twice for the Saints.

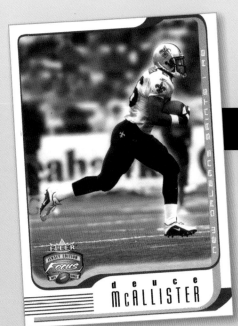

DEUCE MCALLISTER

RUNNING BACK · 2001-2009

Deuce was a big and bruising runner. He was the first Saint to rush for 1,000 yards three years in a row.

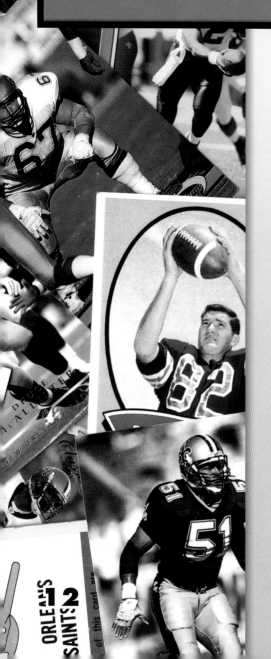

THE BIG PICTURE

Look at the two photos on page 13. Both appear to be the same. But they are not. There are three differences. Can you spot them?

Answers on page 23.

TRUE OR FALSE?

Drew Brees was a star quarterback. Two of these facts about him are **TRUE**. One is **FALSE**. Do you know which is which?

1 Drew was the first NFL player to throw 30 touchdown passes eight years in a row.

2 Drew's nickname is "Cool Brees."

3 Drew was voted Most Valuable Player in the Saints' Super Bowl victory.

Answer on page 23.

Yes! Drew Brees completes another pass.

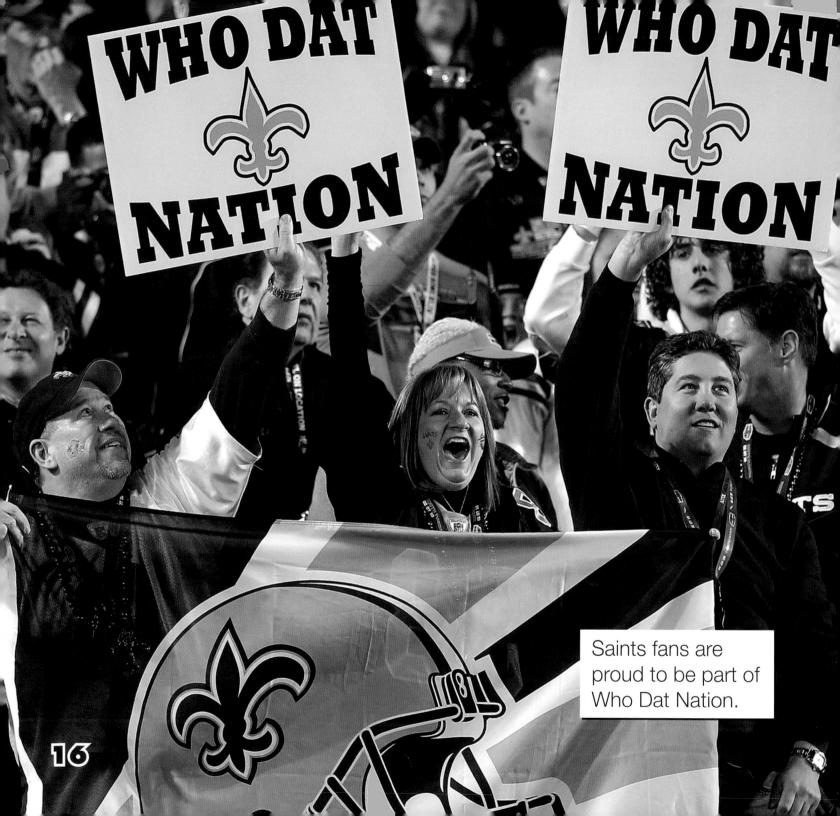

Saints fans are proud to be part of Who Dat Nation.

Go Saints, Go!

New Orleans fans love football as much as they love music. The famous trumpet player Al Hirt was one of the team's first owners. During games, fans often chant, "Who Dat?" It started as a saying by jazz musicians in the city. Saints fans call themselves Who Dat Nation.

ON THE MAP

Here is a look at where five Saints were born, along with a fun fact about each.

1 **SCOTT FUJITA · VENTURA, CALIFORNIA**

Scott was named captain of the team's defense in 2007.

2 **TOM DEMPSEY · MILWAUKEE, WISCONSIN**
In 1970, Tom won a game for the Saints with an amazing 63-yard field goal.

3 **JIMMY GRAHAM · GOLDSBORO, NORTH CAROLINA**
Jimmy caught 51 touchdown passes for the Saints.

4 **SAM MILLS · NEPTUNE, NEW JERSEY**
Sam made the **Pro Bowl** four times for the Saints.

5 **MORTEN ANDERSEN · COPENHAGEN, DENMARK**
Morten led the NFL in field goals in 1987.

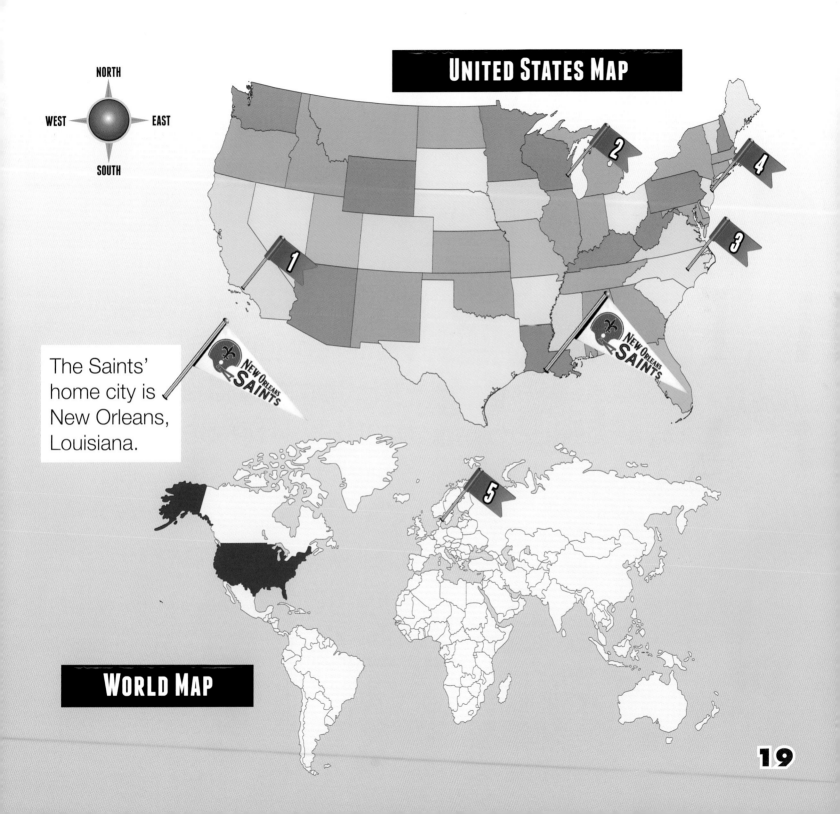

NORTH

WEST   EAST

SOUTH

UNITED STATES MAP

The Saints' home city is New Orleans, Louisiana.

WORLD MAP

Home and Away

Football teams wear different uniforms for home and away games. The Saints have barely changed their uniforms since 1967. Their main colors are gold and black.

Brandin Cooks wears the Saints' home uniform.

Mark Ingram wears the Saints' away uniform.

The Saints' helmet is gold with a black "fleur-de-lis" on each side. That is a French word for "lily." French settlers founded New Orleans in the 1700s.

WE WON!

New Orleans fans waited 33 years for the Saints to win their first game in the **playoffs**. That victory came in 2000. In 2009, the Saints won the Super Bowl for the first time. The offense led the way. But it was a touchdown by defender **Tracy Porter** that sealed the victory.

RECORD BOOK

These Saints set team records.

PASSING YARDS	RECORD
Season: Drew Brees (2011)	5,476
Career: Drew Brees	48,555

RECEIVING YARDS	RECORD
Season: Joe Horn (2004)	1,399
Career: **Marques Colston**	9,759

RUSHING YARDS	RECORD
Season: George Rogers (1981)	1,674
Career: Deuce McAllister	6,096

ANSWERS FOR THE BIG PICTURE
#58's helmet stripe changed colors, #55 changed to #52, and the C on #64's jersey changed to NOLA.

ANSWER FOR TRUE AND FALSE
#2 is false. Drew is not nicknamed "Cool Brees."

FOOTBALL WORDS

INDEX

All-Pro
An honor given to the best NFL player at each position.

Hall of Fame
The museum in Canton, Ohio, where football's greatest players are honored.

Playoffs
The games played after the regular season that decide which teams will play in the Super Bowl.

Pro Bowl
The NFL's annual all-star game.

ABOUT THE AUTHOR

Zack Burgess has been writing about sports for more than 20 years. He has lived all over the country and interviewed lots of All-Pro football players, including Brett Favre, Eddie George, Jerome Bettis, Shannon Sharpe, and Rich Gannon. Zack was the first African American beat writer to cover Major League Baseball when he worked for the *Kansas City Star*.

ABOUT THE SAINTS

Learn more at these websites:
www.neworleanssaints.com • www.profootballhof.com
www.teamspiritextras.com/Overtime/html/saints.html